Haikoons
and the
Dragon Girl

Mewsings on my Feline Flock

by
Carol Rauch

Author & Photographer: Carol Rauch
Book and Cover Designer: Jennifer Tipton Cappoen
Editor: Lynn Bemer Coble

PCBooks is an imprint of **Paws and Claws Publishing, LLC.**
1589 Skeet Club Road, Suite 102-175
High Point, NC 27265
www.PawsandClawsPublishing.com
info@pawsandclawspublishing.com

ISBN #978-1-946198-08-2
Printed in the United States

Carol Rauch

Three fluffy Maine Coons
And a Ragdoll. None of them
Match the carpeting.

Ⓧ

The girls are Lucy
Buttercup, Tosca Mimi,
And Penelope—

Ⓧ

Pearl. The Ragdoll boy
Is Pickwick Fuzzywig. The
Girls are all Maine Coons.

Nose to nose and nose
To toes. I suppose the nose
Knows from nose and toes.

A warm, bright spot of
Sunshine on the rug. I knew
That's where I'd find you.

Penelope
"Snowshoe Kitty"

Carol Rauch

Sleeping. What's that noise?
Oh no! Cat retching. I will
Clean up tomorrow.

Why do you guys have
To growl at each other when
I'm trying to sleep?

Riff-Raff

Mommy's not dressed, yet.
Hurry! Let's open the blinds
And watch Mommy squawk!

What is this I see
On my freshly cleaned rug? Fur
Ball. How fortunate.

Carol Rauch

Under the bed. Tail
Protruding. Just enough to
Let me know she's there.

It's my turn to help
Mommy make the bed. Watch me
Pounce on the wrinkles.

Laundry day! Clean clothes!
Fresh out of the dryer! Still
Covered with cat hair.

Freshly cleaned litter
Boxes. Who will be the first
To make a stinky?

Carol Rauch

Here, Kitty! Kitty!
Come to Mommy! Where are you—
HEY YOU!! Stupid cat.

❋

Here comes Mommy. She
Will want to pick me up and
Cuddle me. Must run.

Tosca Mimi
"Noodles"

My ferocious beast.
Face of a lion. Fangs, claws,
And little pink toes.

Stare down. Ears laid back.
Growling. Tail sweeps the floor. Must
Pause and lick a paw.

Carol Rauch

Mommy has been gone.
For two weeks. We shall ignore
Her when she gets home.

❋

Such a big boy! Such
A little, squeaky meow.
How did that happen?

Pickwick

We are having a
Zen moment: What is the sound
Of one cat napping?

Do you go looking
For Mischief? Or does Mischief
Go looking for you?

Whatcha doing? Are
You playing with air? Oh, I
See. It's a bug's ghost.

Carol Rauch

Two cats wrestling,
Playing vigorously. Must
Stop to lick a paw.

❋

Cat plays with a toy:
Whee! Jump! Pounce! Swat! Sit. Stare. Lick.
Scratch. Whee! Jump! Pounce! Swat….

Riff-Raff

What is this? What do
You mean you don't like it? You
Ate it yesterday.

Somebody tossed their
Cookies. I watch my step as
I go in search. Whoops.

Help me out here. Why
Is that ghastly bug in my
Closet still breathing?

Carol Rauch

Cats speak: What do you
Want to do? I don't know, What
Do you want to do?

❀

I don't know. Why don't
We just sit here at the door
And make Mommy nuts?

Penelope and Lucy

Mommy! Why are you
Screaming at me? I'm only
Playing with the lamp.

Was this once the price-
Less antique vase I got for
A steal on eBay?

Carol Rauch

The world of the Maine
Coon: The cats aren't the only
Things covered in hair.

I don't care if you
Are a Maine Coon. It's cold out.
Get your butt in here.

I already told
You. You may not go outside
And eat a squirrel.

Cats at the window
Watching birds on the feeder.
Feline pastry cart.

Pickwick · Tosca Mimi · Riff-Raff

Carol Rauch

I'm so sorry the
Vet made you toss up that piece
Of yarn you just ate.

Kudos to Dr. Lisa Perez and the staff
at Carolina Veterinary Specialists
for taking care of my
"very sweet and handsome boy."

ME: I spent over two
Hundred bucks to retrieve that
Piece of yarn you ate.

DENISE: Fourteen hundred bucks
And Surgery for the green
Thing Oliver ate.

ANN: Mine ate a gob of
Ribbon. Surgery. The vet
Gave it back to me.

Carol Rauch

I'm trying to sleep.
Fiona* purrs and tickles
Me with her whiskers.

I'm trying to sleep.
In the distance, a noise. Who's
Losing their breakfast?

Fiona
Rest in Peace, Sweet One.

I'm trying to sleep.
Riff-Raff* sits and stares at me.
He has poopy butt.

I'm trying to sleep.
Pickwick bounds across the bed,
Chased by his shadow.

Riff-Raff
Rest in Peace, Sweet One.

Carol Rauch

I'm trying to sleep.
Riff-Raff's splashy-splashy in
The water fountain.

I'm trying to sleep.
In their infinite wisdom,
They open the blinds.

Lucy and Penelope

I'm trying to sleep.
Here comes Puss. He wants to crawl
Under the covers.

I'm trying to sleep.
There goes Puss. He wants out from
Under the covers.

Carol Rauch

I'm trying to sleep.
I have to move over so
Puss can have my spot.

I'm trying to sleep.
Puss has decided to take
Over my pillow.

Figaro
Rest in Peace, Sweet One.

I'm trying to sleep.
It's cold. Someone commandeered
All of the covers.

I'm trying to sleep.
Puss is kneading my ankle.
She is not declawed.

I'm trying to sleep.
Buried under sixty-five
Pounds of cat. Phone rings.

Carol Rauch

Lucy, why do you
Sleep in the litter box? Don't
You know that's nasty?

Lucy, get out of
The box already. Someone
Might need to use it.

DAMMIT, LUCY, GET

YOUR ASS OUT OF THE BOX! No

More kisses for you.

Lucy

Carol Rauch

Fortune cookie say:
Girl with five* cats needs a man
In her life. Chop chop.

❧

Girlfriend say: All good
Men gay or married. Better
Off with the five cats.

*I had five at one time.
There's been some turnover.

Confucius say: She
Who has five cats not getting
Enough attention.

Confucius say: She
Who has five cats need boyfriend.
Not alter kaker. *

Mama say: Screw the
Five cats! When you gonna get
Married already?

* *Yiddish for Old Fart.*

Carol Rauch

Dear Astrologer,
Will I be sleeping with cats
The rest of my life?

Little did I know.

When you touched my heart, you would

Also touch my soul.

Pickwick

DRAGON KING'S DAUGHTER

Sagara, The Dragon King, taught his daughter
   how to swim.
Actually, it came very naturally to her.
Something about the scales. . . .

Anyway, what he could not foresee
Was her penchant for diving.
Into the depths of the sea she would go.
What drew her to swim in the dark and unknown?
Pearls, of course.
Wish-granting jewels.
Each a discovery of beauty and wisdom.
Each one unique, but somehow all the same.
They drew her to them,
But none could keep her.
Each one caught her eye but not her soul.

Then one day, in the deepest and the darkest
   of the sea,
Where she had never ventured before,
She found her most special, radiant Pearl,
The one that touched her heart,
Illuminating all around him.
She begged him to come with her to play in the sun.
She was, after all, the Dragon King's daughter.
She had Dragon daughter duties to tend to up above
And could not spend all her time with her beloved Pearl.
But Pearl had the same problem.
He had Pearl work that kept him
Entrenched in Pearl World.
She could come to him.
He could not go to her.

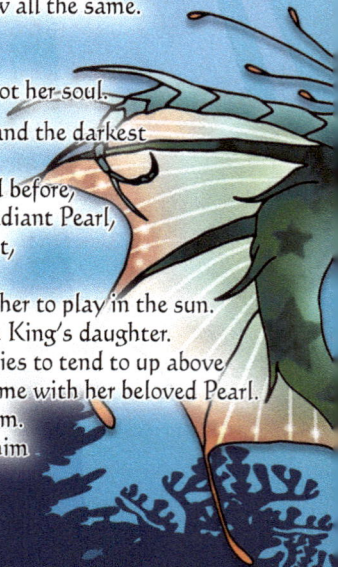

So every day, when Dragon duties were done,
The Dragon King's daughter dove into the depths
    of the sea
To be with her one true Pearl,
Single-mindedly, undistracted, she would find him.
And embrace him.
And lie there, content, in the presence of her Pearl.

After "Mewsings"

Something happened a few years ago. I won't say what it was in a public forum, but if you ask me in person, I'll talk about it.

I cried every day for months. You would think someone had died. My friends weren't used to seeing me like this. I wasn't used to seeing me like this. Confronted with my sadness, I decided I would challenge my situation with my heart this time, not with my head, which was my usual way of maintaining sanity. In my process, I began to seek a greater understanding of the big picture, which led me to embark on deepening my connection to "Spirit."

In the midst of crying every day for months, I began to write these "Haikoons" to cheer myself up. I also decided I needed to write about what it was that happened and, surprisingly, I did it through poetry. Writing poetry is not my thing, but four poems managed to work their way out of me. Actually, they wrote themselves. Together, they tell the story. But since I'm not ready to tell the story here, I'm only including the last one. The one about hope.

I am a Nichiren Buddhist. Nam-Myoho-Renge-Kyo is my spiritual anchor. It is my prayer. My job is to offer it to the Universe, the forces that be, and then get out of the way. My journey into deepening my connection to Spirit led me to begin reading *The Lotus Sutra and Its Opening and Closing Sutras,* translated by Burton Watson. That's where we find the image of the Dragon King's Daughter.

The Dragon King's Daughter is significant for three reasons. First, she's a she, the first female character in all the Buddhist sutras to become enlightened. Second, she's only eight years old. She hasn't spent countless years learning how to be who and what she is not or trying to achieve some unrealistic level of perfection. That leads me to the third point, which is, she is a dragon. In the infinitely loving and creative mind of the Universe, regardless of who and what she is, her life is of immeasurable value.

I found out in recent years dragons have a thing for pearls. So *Pearl* for me has come to represent the heart's desire. Fearlessly, in defiance of those who would malign her, the Dragon King's Daughter offered her Pearl to The World-Honored One, who accepted it without hesitation.

Then she became a Buddha.

About the Author

Carol Rauch earned her Bachelor of Arts in Psychology from the University of North Carolina in Chapel Hill in December 1980, a Bachelor of Arts in Music from Guilford College in May 1992, and a Master of Arts in Liberal Studies from the University of North Carolina in

Photo Credit: Lori Polena

Greensboro in May 2000. Currently, she is a property owner/manager and does some editing work on the side. So far, her editing work has included two novels, a couple of nonfiction books, some articles and newsletters, poetry, a memoir, and one dissertation.

The author's interests include knitting, needlework, and the performing arts. She specializes in unfinished projects! She relishes being of service to her four cats and is also an avid Mah-Jongg™ player.

Carol has been a professional harpist for over 30 years. She performs with the Philharmonia of Greensboro, the Danville

Symphony, the Salem Community Orchestra, and the Piedmont Wind Symphony. She also performs in an annual production of *The Wizard of Oz* with the Community Theatre of Greensboro, which she has been doing for 22 years. She freelances for weddings, funerals, church services, and special events. Carol continues to take lessons on the harp and is the first to say the learning process never ends.

Carol became a Nichiren Buddhist in 1978. She will always be a spiritual seeker. Buddhism is her anchor. The work never ends.

To my Pearl.

www.ingramcontent.com/pod-product-compliance
Lightning Source LLC
LaVergne TN
LVHW010305070426
835508LV00026B/3441